American Legends: The Life of Doris Day

By Charles River Editors

Doris Day in 1960

About Charles River Editors

Charles River Editors was founded by Harvard and MIT alumni to provide superior editing and original writing services, with the expertise to create digital content for publishers across a vast range of subject matter. In addition to providing original digital content for third party publishers, Charles River Editors republishes civilization's greatest literary works, bringing them to a new generation via ebooks.

Introduction

Doris Day in 1953

Doris Day (1924-)

"I've been through everything. I always said I was like those round-bottomed circus dolls — you know, those dolls you could push down and they'd come back up? I've always been like that. I've always said, 'No matter what happens, if I get pushed down, I'm going to come right back up.'" – Doris Day

A lot of ink has been spilled covering the lives of history's most influential figures, but how much of the forest is lost for the trees? In Charles River Editors' American Legends series, readers can get caught up to speed on the lives of America's most important men and women in the time it takes to finish a commute, while learning interesting facts long forgotten or never known.

It goes without saying that few people have a career spanning 8 decades, yet that claim to fame is occupied by the legendary Doris Day, who got her start in show business as a singer in a big band in 1939 and has not let up since. From there, Day went on to record dozens of albums and hundreds of songs, winning a countless number of awards on the way to being one of the 20th century's most popular singers. One of those recognitions came just a few years ago in 2011, when Day, by that time nearing 90 years old, released a new album that charted 9th in the UK Top 40 Albums, making her the oldest singer ever with that distinction.

Her musical career would've been impressive enough, but Doris Day is just as well known today for her film career, which wasn't so bad itself. Though her time in Hollywood was much shorter in comparison to her music career, she nevertheless managed to reach the top in that industry as well. As one of the most popular actresses of the '60s, Day was the biggest box office draw in Hollywood in the early half of that decade, and the only woman among the Top 10. In the process of making nearly 40 movies, Day would eventually be recognized as the highest grossing actress in history, and at the same time she was good enough at her craft to be nominated for an Oscar for Best Actress.

Amazingly, despite her incredible success in both music and film, Day eventually found herself bankrupt due to the mismanagement of her money by her husband, compelling her to reinvent herself as the host of a popular television sitcom. Perhaps not surprisingly, Day excelled in this field as well, making *The Doris Day Show* one of the most popular shows on television for several years at the end of the '60s.

American Legends: The Life of Doris Day examines the life and career of one of the entertainment industry's biggest stars. Along with pictures of important people, places, and events, you will learn about Doris Day like never before, in no time at all.

Chapter 1: Dawn of Day

Young Doris

"It is my nature to forgive, to try to accentuate what is good, and not to pass judgment. I am often make sorrowful by the disappointment and disillusionment I have suffered in people, but hate her condemnation is not part of it." – Doris Day

On April 3, 1924, Doris Mary Ann Kappelhoff was the first daughter born to first-generation Americans Alma Sophia Welz and William Kappelhoff. A few decades before her birth, all four of the young girl's grandparents had come to America from Germany and settled in Cincinnati, Ohio. During that time it was common for people who came to America from other countries to live in neighborhoods with others from the same country, and in Cincinnati there were several ethnic neighborhoods, including a German section, Russian section, and Polish section among others. Doris's maternal grandparents, the Welz's, and her paternal grandparents, the Kappelhoff's, raised families near each other, so it was no surprise when their children met and married.

Before Doris was born, Sophia and William had two boys, but the first, Richard, died before Doris was born, so she was raised in the house with only Paul, who was several years older. From the beginning, the Kappelhoff's were a musical family; William was a music teacher, and the house was always full of his piano, violin, and music theory students coming and going for lessons. William was also the organist at St. Mark's Catholic Church, where the family faithfully attended mass.

Like many gifted men, William was quiet and introverted, but Alma, on the other hand, loved company, music and parties. Unlike her husband, who preferred classical music, Alma loved traditional American fare, including hillbilly and country-western pieces. She also loved the movies and named her daughter after her favorite movie star: Doris Kenyon. Many years later, Doris Day would buy a house just a few houses down from her namesake.

Doris Kenyon

As a young child, Doris was a little high-strung, as well as very creative and imaginative. As a result she often had nightmares, and as a young girl, she would run to her parents' room for comfort, only to be told by her father to go back to bed and control herself. She would then stand outside their door quietly sniffling until her mother tiptoed out and carried her back to bed. The two would snuggle there together until Doris, feeling safe and secure, would fall back asleep. Given that, it is no surprise that Doris grew up as a classic "mama's girl", and while her imagination plagued her in the darkness, it provided her no end of wholesome entertainment during the day. She spent a lot of her free time alone, with her older brother at school and no sisters to play with, so she played with her dolls and played house.

The family lived in a red brick duplex at the corner of Jonathan and Greenlawn Streets in the German section of Cincinnati, and since they grew up in the area, William and Alma had plenty of friends. In addition to hosting parties, the family often joined others in the local beer garden for music food and games, and even as a young child, the people living around Doris sensed that she would one day be famous. Foremost among them was Alma, who supported her daughter's efforts and encouraged her to pursue her singing and dancing. Doris would later say, "I always felt that she was vicariously having this thrill through me. My mother was an adorable lady and I think that she would have liked performing. When I mentioned this to her, she'd say 'Oh, no. I didn't want you to do it for that reason.' And I say, 'Oh, I don't know about that. I think so.' But she never admitted to that."

Doris and Alma

Hoping that her daughter had inherited some of her father's musical talent, Alma arranged for young Doris to take piano lessons, but Doris did not enjoy playing the piano, perhaps because the music reminded her of her distant and absent father. After that failed endeavor, when Doris was old enough to start kindergarten, Alma sent her to Pep Golden's Dance School, where Doris worked hard and practiced for her big debut in her first recital.

However, things did not go as planned. Only five years old, Doris was one of the youngest performers and was terribly nervous before performing. By the time her turn had come to go on stage, she had wet her pants, with a large spot staining the front of her red satin skirt. She bravely went on stage and began to perform her part as the audience tried to keep from laughing, but when she saw her mother, she burst into tears and began to tell her how sorry she was. Doris later recalled with pride that, in spite of her humiliation, she remembered to make a ladylike curtsy before she ran off the stage.

Instead of blaming her daughter for lack of self-control, Alma blamed the school for not preparing Doris properly for her role. As a result, She withdrew Doris from Golden's and sent her instead to Shuster Marten's school. Now at a new school, Doris thrived, studying ballet, singing, public speaking, and acrobatics. Her hard work paid off when she won first prize in standing on her hands, and the prize, 25 free lessons, enabled her to continue at the school.

Accustomed to being alone, Doris spent her time after school doing homework, taking lessons and entering contests, but her life was turned upside down when she was 8. During a party at her parents' home, she overheard something that she would later realize was her father having an affair with her mother's best friend. Confused and afraid of the ramifications, she kept it secret well into her adulthood, worried that if she told her mother, there would be trouble. As it turned out, there was trouble anyway, because William was eventually caught. Alma was embarrassed, William was fired by the church, and Doris's parents separated shortly after. To make matters worse, when her father left, he stopped and said goodbye to Paul but didn't even bother trying to find Doris and say goodbye. Doris witnessed his departure from behind the drapes in the living room.

At first, Alma might have hoped that William, being a devout Catholic, would return to the family, but as time went on, it became obvious that this was not going to happen. The couple divorced in 1936, and Alma moved with her children to College Hill, a Cincinnati suburb where she worked at the Evanston Bakery in order to support herself and her children. For his part, William stayed in touch by picking up the children on Wednesday evenings and taking them to his sister's home for dinner. Doris would later compliment her family, saying, "I had a wonderful family including my aunts, uncles and cousins…"

When the family moved to College Hill, Alma enrolled Doris at our Lady of Angels School, and as was common at the time, the school regularly held talent shows. Naturally, Doris entered them all, and during one of the shows, she turned to a woman and commented that the boy who was dancing on stage was "cute". That woman, who was the boy's mother, appreciated the young girl's comments and decided to introduce the two. Doris and the boy got along well, so they decided to work up a dance routine to do together, and that is how Jerry Doherty became Doris Day's first dance partner. Their routine, "Clouds", soon became a crowd favorite at every church function and benefit where they performed.

Doris and Jerry

When the new school year began in the fall of 1936, a local department store held a dance contest, and Doris and Jerry decided to enter it. They spent several weekends over the next several months competing against hundreds of other contestants at a local radio studio, and in the end, they won $500 for their routine, "The Funny Little Bird on Nellie's Hat." After much discussion, the parents decided that the money should be used for Doris and Jerry to go to Hollywood; Alma and Mrs. Darby would make the trip with the children, while Mr. Darby stayed home and prepared to possibly sell his dairy business. Throughout the spring and summer of 1937, the pair continued to perform locally in order to earn more money for the trip.

Chapter 2: Day and Night

"I'm still Doris Mary Keppellhoff from Cincinnati, Ohio. All I ever wanted to do was to get married, have a nice husband, have two or three children, keep house and cook – a nice clean house – and live happily ever after – and I ended up in Hollywood. And if I can do it, you can do it. Anyone can do it." – Doris Day

Finally, the big day came. In July 1937, Alma, Doris, and Jerry's family left Cincinnati and turned west toward California. When they arrived, they rented a small apartment together for one month, and the mothers went immediately to the Louis DePron's dance school and enrolled the children in lessons. DePron was impressed, and he soon had the young pair performing around the area.

It was during this time that Doris almost had her big break. She and Jerry were studying at Fanshon and Marco's when a talent scout from Paramount Studios spotted her and thought she could be an actress. He approached her and offered her a screen test, but Doris turned him down because she was not willing to break her partnership agreement with Jerry. The studio representative had a hard time understanding why she would turn down such a chance, but she replied that she did not want to be an actress, "not if it might hurt somebody else."

By the end of July, everyone agreed that the two teenagers had enough talent to justify staying in Hollywood permanently. Thus, they went back to Cincinnati to sell their homes and pack up their belongings. By the first of October, Mr. Darby had sold his business, and the two families had rented an apartment in Los Angeles. However, tragedy nearly struck less than two weeks later. On Friday the 13th, Doris and her mother went to a farewell party in Hamilton, a small town about 25 miles from Cincinnati, and while there, the phone rang and Doris found out that Jerry's brother Larry, with whom she was going steady, had a couple of friends that also wanted to say goodbye. Thus, Larry and Doris went with another couple, Albert Schroeder and Marion Bonehamp, to a nearby café for a quick bite to eat, after which they headed back to the party, with Albert driving and Marion in the front seat with him. Doris was seated behind Albert, with Larry in the back passenger seat.

According to Doris' later recollection, it was a cold rainy night and the windows fogged over. They were carefully driving along a country road when the four suddenly saw a flash of light bearing down on them. They had somehow come across a train track and were hit once by the locomotive and then again when the car spun into the side of the train. Though Albert and Marion went through the windshield, no one was killed, probably due to the heavy duty makeup of 1930s automobiles. However, Doris was seriously injured, and when she was rushed to Mercy Hospital, she was diagnosed with a double compound fracture and bone fragments in her right leg. As she lay on a gurney preparing to go into surgery, she was praying that she would one day be able to dance again, while the doctors working on her were just hoping that she would one day be able to walk.

During the surgery, the doctors were able to insert a steel pin into her leg and set it with a long cast from her thigh to her toes. They assured her that she would likely be able to walk perfectly well when the cast came off, but dancing might be a different story. In the meantime, Jerry and Doris's Hollywood dreams were crushed. They disbanded the act, and both of them returned to the local high school. Doris soon dropped out of school once it proved too much for her to hobble on crutches to the three different streetcars required to get to classes. Even if she did get to classes, there was always the danger that someone would accidentally trip her. As a result, she decided to stay home for the four months it would take for her leg to fully heal.

Unfortunately, four months stretched into 14 months when Doris tripped over a rug and fell again, re-fracturing the leg. Nevertheless, throughout her recovery, Doris remained optimistic and spent her time singing along with to the radio by her bed. She would later say, "During this long, boring period, I used to while away a lot of time listening to the radio, sometimes singing along with the likes of Benny Goodman, Duke Ellington, Tommy Dorsey and Glenn Miller. But the one radio voice I listened to above others belonged to Ella Fitzgerald. There was a quality to her voice that fascinated me, and I'd sing along with her, trying to catch the subtle ways she shaded her voice, the casual yet clean way she sang the words."

Still committed to encouraging her daughter's talent, Alma encouraged Doris take voice lessons, but Doris did not care for her first voice coach and classically trained musician, who likely reminded her of her father. Undeterred, Alma soon arranged for Doris to study with Grace Raine, a popular music teacher who taught Doris, "When you sing, don't think of a big audience. Sing into someone's ear – a person. You're acting." Doris would later say, "That training helped me immeasurably year later when I became as actress." When Raine learned that Alma was taking up sewing in order to pay for Doris' lesson, she offered to reduce her price for the lessons by 66%, and even while she was still on crutches, Doris also began pitching in on her lessons by earning $5 an evening for singing at Charlie Yee's Shanghai Inn. Raine was also able to get Doris on WLW radio's Carlin's Carnival, though she was not paid for this role.

More than just Doris's career was shaped during this time; she also became a passionate animal lover thanks to the devotion of Tiny, a small black and tan dog that remained by her side throughout her recovery. When he was tragically hit by a car and killed, Doris was inconsolable, and she later devoted her life to animal rights causes.

In 1939, Barney Rapp, a local bandleader, held auditions for a new girl singer, and after hearing Doris sing on Carlin's Carnival, he encouraged her to try out for the position. In the end, she beat out over 200 other singers to get her first steady job as a performer. Her starting salary was $50 per week, but the band manager secretly kept half of it for himself; Doris was too young and naïve to realized how little she was being paid. Since she was still only 16 years old, Doris also had to lie about her age and claim to be 18 in order to legally work at nightclubs.

Barney Rapp

In addition to falsifying Doris's age, Rapp also persuaded her to change her name, and after hearing her perform "Day After Day", Rapp had Doris change her last name from the memorable but hard to pronounce Kappelhoff to the simple and elegant Day. Thus, when she was finally introduced, it was Doris Day who was the new female vocalist for Rapp and the New Englanders.

At first, Alma drove Doris to the club each night, but she became increasingly embarrassed to be seen with her mother, as most girls her age do. Eventually, she asked 23 year old trombonist Al Jorden to give her a ride to work each night, despite the fact she had such a low opinion of him that she once told her mother, "He's a creep and I wouldn't go out with him if they were giving away gold nuggets at the movie!" However, even though she could barely stand Jorden at first, the two subsequently fell in love. Unfortunately, Day was too young to recognize Jorden's problems, especially his jealousy and irrational temper. Once, when they were out boating with another couple, Jorden gunned the boat's engine so hard that the boat flipped, requiring them to be rescued by *Cincinnati Times Star* reporter Jerry Hurter. Not surprisingly, their accident and the tale of the rescue were on the front page of the paper the next day.

When Rapp's nightclub closed, he took the band, and Doris, on the road, so for the next several months, she endured night after long night of single location gigs. This routine exhausted the young teen, who began looking for work elsewhere, and eventually she went to work for Bob Crosby in Chicago for $75 a week. Though she remained with the band for only three months, she still got to make her first Broadway appearance performing at the Strand Theater before she was let go once Crosby's former singer, Bonnie King, returned. After leaving Crosby, Day soon found more work performing with Fred Waring, and then she joined Les Brown on tour in 1940, appearing with Gypsy Rose Lee. Though she and Brown released several singles during this time, none were hits.

Chapter 3: Long Days

"I always felt that making a living wasn't the easiest thing in the world, and I decided I was going straight ahead and try to be as uncomplicated as possible. The important thing in life is just living and loving." – Doris Day

Just days after her 17th birthday, Day made one of her most fateful decisions. Al Jorden had come back into her life and proposed, and Day would later recall, "It was the happiest time that I could ever have. But that's when I stopped my career." Not surprisingly, everyone from her mother to the guys in the band told Day she was making a mistake; even Jorden's own mother warned the girl against marrying her son. However, like so many 17 year old girls, her heart drowned out all voices of reason.

Alma was worried about Doris's decision, but she wanted to at least make sure that her daughter really got married and wouldn't just be "shacking up", so she drove Doris to New York. There, between Jorden's daily performances with Jimmy Dorsey, the two were married at the New York City Hall. They then moved into a small apartment in the Whitby building.

Day's marriage to Jorden started off badly and quickly got worse, as she would later explain: "We had a correspondence courtship and it was not good. I do not recommend it. We got married and we really didn't know each other." She would later add, "Had we been together more, I wouldn't have married him." This is certainly true, because if they had been together she would have realized how out of control his jealousy was. They had only been married two days when he beat her for the first time; the newlyweds had just returned from meeting his friends in the band, and he somehow got it in his head that she had been cheating on him.

When he calmed down, Jorden apologized to Day and promised never to hit her again. Young, in love, afraid and embarrassed that she had not listened to everyone's warning, Day chose to believe him. Not surprisingly, this proved to be a mistake because Jorden's promise was worthless. He continued to beat Doris periodically throughout the first months of their marriage, and just as she decided that she had to get out of the marriage, Day discovered that she was pregnant. With no money to get back home, she decided to stay with him until the baby was born and she could earn enough to make her way back to Cincinnati.

At first, it seemed that impending fatherhood might have stabilized Jorden's moods, but one day, while they were in the car together, he became enraged and put a loaded gun to her head. He then tried to force her to have an abortion, and when Doris refused, Jorden eventually tried to abort their baby himself by beating her worse than ever before. Day finally found a way out when she and Jorden travelled with Dorsey to Chicago. As they passed through Cincinnati, Jorden allowed her to visit her family with the caveat that she not tell anyone she was pregnant. By this time, however, she was showing, and her mother guessed her condition. When she was told about Jorden's desire for an abortion, Alma was so enraged that she threatened to kill Jorden herself if Doris got an abortion.

When Jorden found out that Doris had told her parents, he flew into a rage and accused her of telling everyone. He even beat her one evening at his parents' house, and his mother heard it and demanded that he stop. She then questioned Doris about what was going on, but instead of being sympathetic, she observed that Doris didn't look too badly beaten. The next day, Doris returned to her own mother's home and confided in her that she was in trouble. Alma begged her to stay with her, but Doris insisted that she would return to Cincinnati as soon as her baby was born, so Alma went to stay with her daughter and was there when her son, Terrence "Terry" Jorden, was born. When Day went into labor, Alma tried to reach Jorden to tell him the birth was imminent but was unable to reach him, and when he returned home, she found out why. She found a note from another woman in his pocket, but she ultimately chose not to tell Doris about it.

While Doris adored her new son and was determined to be a good mother, Jorden showed little interest in the baby, even going so far as to claim the kid wasn't hit. He continued to be abusive and even followed Day to Cincinnati when her mother rented her a house there, living with his family for awhile. Finally, Doris had enough; one day, she waited until he left the house and then had all the locks changed. She filed for divorce the next day.

Despite how awful her first marriage had been, Day remained optimistic, explaining, "One beautiful thing came out of that marriage, and that was my son, and if I hadn't married this bird, I wouldn't have my terrific son, Terry. So you see, out of these awful experiences come something terrific."

Chapter 4: Day's Break

"I don't see my films – I see all the wrong things I've done and I turn them off. But sometimes a song will come on the radio. A song I've done a long time ago – and I think 'ahhh' and I'll listen – really listen – and I'll feel so good inside and say: 'I did it.'" – Doris Day

During the months immediately following her divorce from Jorden, Doris Day learned a lesson that would carry her well through many of life's difficulties: hard work is an excellent comfort for a broken heart. In many ways, she had no choice but to work hard, since she now had no husband, no money and a child to support. She was back home living with her mother, but even though she and Alma were always close, it was obviously not a permanent situation.

Naturally, Doris returned to what she did know, so as soon as she could, she returned to performing. Not wanting to leave her son, she at first refused to go on road trips, instead getting a job singing for 15 minutes five evenings a week on the local Cincinnati radio station WLW. Eventually, Les Brown heard her on one of these shows and begged her to come back to his band, and after much soul searching, she agreed. Leaving young Terry with her mother, she began traveling with the band again, making good money but rarely sleeping in the same city two nights in a row.

Les Brown

Then her life changed with one song. In 1944, the band began rehearsing a new number called "Sentimental Journey." Everyone liked it, and Day sounded like an angel singing the lead, but it was the lyrics and haunting melody that would make the song a hit with war weary servicemen and their families:

"Gonna take a sentimental journey

Gonna set my heart at ease

Gonna make a sentimental journey

To renew old memories

Got my bag

Got my reservation

Spent each dime

I could afford

Like a child

In wild anticipation

Long to hear that

All aboard"

By the time the song was released in January 1945, there wasn't a family in America that wasn't longing for someone to make a "sentimental journey" home. The song went to the top of the record charts and remained the number one song in America for 9 weeks.

Fittingly, "Sentimental Journey" also made Doris Day a hit, and over the next year, she and the band would record six more hits. The first, "My Dreams Are Getting Better All the Time," also made the billboard charts, as did "You Won't Be Satisfied (Until You Break My Heart)" and "The Whole World is Singing My Song." Finally, "I Got the Sun in the Mornin'," from the musical *Annie Get Your Gun*, made the charts in the spring of 1946. By the time Day left the band in August 1946, she was the highest paid "girl singer" in the world.

Just as Day found work to be a comfort for a broken heart, she also seemed to find falling in love to be an interesting diversion. Just as she had with Al Jorden, Day again married a man she was working with, this time George Weilder, who she married on March 30, 1946. Like Jorden, Weilder was a musician in Brown's band, playing the saxophone, and it was at his urging that she left the group; when he wanted to go to Los Angeles and join a new band there, she went with him.

As it turned out, moving to California at this point in her career was helpful. She first got a job singing with Bob Hope for CBS Radio, and when they dropped her, she signed a contract to record songs for Columbia Records. Day also signed an agent, Al Levy, who knew his way around the business well enough to get her booked to sing at Billy Reed's Little Club back in

New York. Thus, she went across the country, while her new husband stayed behind to pursue his career on the West Coast. The New Yorkers at Billy Reed's liked Day, and the management offered to extend her contract for $150 per week for another four weeks.

Bob Hope

Unfortunately, Day felt like she was in no position to accept the offer, because she had received a "Dear Jane letter" from Weilder saying that he wanted a divorce. Being a performer himself, he sensed that she was about to make it big and did not want to live the rest of his life in her shadow. However, since she feared the stigma of being a "two time loser", Day flew back to Los Angeles to try to save her marriage, only for Weilder to tell her he was not interested in repairing their relationship. Day was devastated, and despite the fact they officially separated in April 1947, she did not file for divorce until 14 months later.

At first, Day planned to return to Cincinnati and move back in with her mother and son, figuring she could stay there and lick her wounds while she regrouped, but shortly before she left Los Angeles, she was invited to sing at a party at the home of popular composer Jule Styne. Day sang "Embraceable You" and impressed her hostess, as well as Sammie Cahn. They were both working for Warner Brothers at that time and insisted that she do a screen test for their new film, *Romance on the High Seas*.

Day was not enthusiastic, and her screen test became the stuff of Hollywood legend. Director Michael Curtiz, who had risen to fame for his direction of *Casablanca,* was directing the test, which would have intimidated most women, but Day didn't care. She was too broken up over her marriage to stop crying; she would get herself under control, begin to sing and then start sobbing again. A compassionate man, Curtiz decided to try to reason with Day and encourage her to do her best. He began to question her about her acting experience, only to hear her sigh, "I've never acted. I don't know a thing about acting." Startled at her honesty, he asked if she even wanted to be an actress. Again, she responded with frightening honesty: "Oh, I suppose. I guess it might be interesting." She then went on to tell Curtiz about her family problems and about how she really just wanted to go home to Cincinnati.

Curtiz

Comforted by Curtiz's kind interest, Day began to pull herself together and ask what part he wanted her to play. When he told her he wanted her to play the lead, Doris was shocked and cried out, "How can I possible be the lead? I haven't had any experience – I don't know how to act. That seems pretty crazy to me." Barely controlling his laughter, Curtiz gently replied, "You let me decide that." He then told her to go home and rest and come back the next day for the screen test.

The screen test itself proved to be even more astonishing. Day handled it like a pro and later commented that she "felt a nice exhilaration at hearing the word 'Action!' and then responding to the pressure of the rolling camera." For his part, Curtiz was amazed by her poise and professionalism. He told someone, "It was not like an actress reading. This was something I was not used to. The little lady read like a human being...."

In spite of her success at the screen test, Day still planned on returning to Cincinnati, but ultimately, a personal phone call from the film's star, Jack Carson, convinced her to stay and actually make the movie.

Carson in 1943

Chapter 5: Laughing and Singing All Day

"[Comedy is] harder because it's not real. Drama is real – that life, and you react as in life and that you don't have to think about timing so much better in comedy, timing is everything. If you try to be funny, you will never be funny. I have to play comedy very real. If this situation is funny, you play it absolutely totally real. People sit back and say, "Make me laugh. Now make me laugh more. Now make me laugh really hard. Now make me laugh even harder," and if they're not screaming when they go out, they say, that wasn't so hot. But with real-life drama, if they shed a few tears, that's okay. It's much easier." – Doris Day

Day soon learned just how hard a comedy was to make. Though *Romance on the High Seas* was written by the famous Epstein brothers, the screenwriters who had written *Casablanca*, it was more silly than truly funny. In the movie, Day played Georgia Garrett, a young woman hired by a jealous wife to replace her on a cruise so that the wife can use her time on land to prove that her husband is cheating on her. Meanwhile, the husband has hired a private detective, played by Jack Carson, to follow his wife on the ship. Farce ensues when the detective falls in love with Garrett, leading the husband and wife to reconcile. In the pattern of the 1940s romantic comedy, both couples ultimately live happily ever after.

Day in *Romance on the High Seas*

The best that can be said about *Romance on the High Seas* is that it was pretty standard fare, and certainly not the kind of vehicle that would provide a breakthrough for a new actress. While her acting at this time was nothing to write home about, Day stood out by singing two musical numbers in the film, and fortunately, Curtiz realized that any problems with the movie were due to the script, not the new actress. Warner Bros. agreed, to the extent that the studio subsequently gave her a 7 year contract. Delighted to finally have steady work that required no significant travel, Day sent for Alma and Terry and moved them in with her into her own home in Hollywood.

For the next seven years, Day continued to work during the day filming musicals for Warner Bros. and come home to her mother and son at night. Though this was a domestically happy era in her life, professionally it was only mediocre. Most of the musicals that Day made for Warner Bros. were nearly as silly as *Romance on the High Seas*, and they all followed the same premise: slightly humorous plot, adequate acting, and decent costuming, all highlighted by Day's singing. Of course, there were some exceptions; for example, *Young Man with a Horn* allowed Day to draw on her own life experiences to play Jo Jorden, a "girl singer" working during the big band era. The film itself is slightly semi-autobiographical, based on Dorothy Baker's fictionalized telling of the life of jazz musician Bix Beiderbecke.

Day's acting was always based on her own sense of how to speak and move, rather than some sort of method of getting into the mind of the character she was playing. This shines through in

Young Man with a Horn, as she moves with ease across the stage and interacts with other members of the band. This is a life she understood, and it shows. According to one author, "... *Young Man with a Horn* served the important function of alerting viewers of the fact that Doris Day was an actress of surprising talent and capable of playing much more than the simple girl next door."

Given the drama of her personal life, Doris Day was certainly not the girl next door, but that image would prove to be the bread and butter of her acting career. In 1950, she was voted the favorite star of American soldiers stationed in Korea, and it goes without saying that most of them had no clue the girl of their dreams was actually a 25 year old twice-divorced mother of a 7 year old boy. In fact, it was indeed Day's ability to remain innocent looking and young no matter what life threw at her that shaped not only her acting career but her personal life too. She would later say, "I like joy; I want to be joyous. I want to smile and I want to make people laugh. And that's all I want. I like being happy. I want to make others happy."

Day went on to make one musical after another for Warner Bros, and one of these, *The West Point Story*, cast her alongside film legend James Cagney. Cagney played a Broadway director hired to put on a show for West Point, and Day played one of the young women cast in the show. Cagney always referred to himself as a "song and dance man", and he and Day performed well on screen together, but the film's premise bothered some critics, and the movie only did moderately well in the box office.

One of Day's more outstanding musicals for Warner Bros. was *On Moonlight Bay*, in which she plays Marjorie, the tomboy daughter of a 1920s family living in small-town Indiana. Of course, she falls for the boy next door, and to win him over, she tries to transform herself into a more lady-like figure in the hopes of winning his heart. In spite of her best efforts, her father still doesn't approve, and it appears that the two will never get together, but like most Hollywood endings, the two young lovers are united at the end of the movie.

Three years later, Day starred in the sequel to *On Moonlight Bay*. Like the original, *By the Light of the Silvery Moon* was named for a popular 1930s love song, and this movie begins with Marjorie's boyfriend returning from World War I. Just like the old saying that the course of true love never runs smoothly, the couple goes through all sorts of problems before ultimately reaching the happy ending. Naturally, there are several musical ballads sung by Day throughout the course of the film.

Doris Day in *Starlift* (1951)

"Middle age is youth without levity, and age without decay…The really frightening thing about middle age is the knowledge that you'll grow out of it." – Doris Day

While Middle America soon came to love Day and flocked to see her pictures, her first real blockbuster was *I'll See You in My Dreams*. The movie, released in 1951, was one of a genre particularly popular during the 1950s: the musical biopic. In it, Day plays Grace Kahn, the wife of popular Hollywood songwriter Gus Kahn (played by Danny Thomas). Day was under a certain amount of unusual pressure in this role because Mrs. Khan was still alive at the time of filming, but she was ultimately pleased with Day's portrayal of her life, and she was probably flattered to be played by the attractive actress with golden blond hair. Day and Thomas worked well together too, singing and dancing across the screen to "My Buddy" and "Toot Toot Tootsie". The public loved the film so much that it became the second highest grossing film in 1952.

In 1953, Doris made one of the most popular films of her early career: Calamity Jane. A tongue in cheek look at one of the Old West's most famous women, the Western musical featured Day's rendition of "Secret Love", which won the Academy award that year for Best Original Song. It also became Day's first single to go to the top of America's Billboard chart, and by this time, albums from any of Day's movies were likely to hit the charts somewhere. Six of the soundtracks from her movies made it to the top 10 spot, and three of them eventually reached number one.

Doris Day as Calamity Jane

Day finished her contract with Warner Bros. by filming two musicals in 1954. In the first of these, *Lucky Me*, she co-starred with Phil Silvers, one of Hollywood's classic comedians. While working with Silvers no doubt improved her comedic timing, her next film, *Young at Heart*, gave her a chance to improve her musical performance by working with the legendary Frank Sinatra.

Day had personal reasons for not renewing her contract with Warner Bros. In 1951, she had married for a third time, and this time, Marty Melcher proved to be the man she had always been looking for. For one thing, he wanted to be a good father to Terry, going so far as to adopt the boy. For another, Melcher was a skilled producer who was devoted to Day's career. Together, the two formed Arwin Productions in 1952, and for the rest of Melcher's life, the company was devoted to producing movies starring Day.

Day and Melcher

In spite of her acting success, or perhaps because of it, Day was not at this time interested in appearing on television. Furthermore, now that she was finally happily married, she was more interested in spending time with her family than in putting in more hours in front of the camera. However, in 1954 she appeared on the popular television game show *What's My Line?* By using a squeaky, cartoonish voice, she was able to keep the three blindfolded panelists from recognizing her for most of the show. Finally, veteran panelist Arlene Francis guessed her identity after the eighth question.

While many celebrities appeared on that show, Day's appearance was significant because she appeared to be as comfortable in front of a live studio audience as she was on screen. She had gotten her start singing before an audience, but she had not been performing in front of a live audience for almost a decade. Nevertheless, her connection with people was still just as strong, and her comfort in this setting would come in handy a decade later.

As the 1950s wore on, Day began to expand her acting horizons. In 1955, she starred in another biopic, *Love Me or Leave Me*, again co-starring with James Cagney. This time she was playing the subject of the film, singer Ruth Etting, and Cagney was the spouse. In Day's opinion, *Love Me or Leave Me* was her best film, and others agreed. The film was both a critical and financial success, and naturally, the movie's soundtrack album went straight to the top of the charts and stayed there for 28 weeks. In fact, it ended up being the third most popular soundtrack of the 1950s.

Doris Day in the trailer for *Love Me or Leave Me*

Following the success of *Love Me or Leave Me*, Day went on to play Jimmy Stewart's wife in one of Alfred Hitchcock's classic mystery film, *The Man Who Knew Too Much*. Released in 1956, this movie featured Day crooning what would become her signature melody, "Que Sera, Sera" to her young son. The song was an immediate hit, and that year, "Que Sera, Sera" won an Oscar for best original song.

It took a lot of courage for Day to work with Hitchcock, who had a reputation for being one of the most demanding and particular directors in Hollywood at the time. As filming continued, she became increasingly concerned with his lack of comment on her performance. When she finally spoke with him about this, he replied in his typical way, "If you weren't doing what I liked, you'd know." He later told a reporter that he took no credit for how well Day performed on camera, saying, "It wasn't me; it was Doris."

By this time, Doris Day began to believe that she could play dramatic roles just as easily as she did comedy, but she quickly learned otherwise when she made *Julie* in 1956. *Julie* was both a critical and a box office flop, though film critic Dennis Schwartz noted, "Doris Day, to her credit, gives it her best shot and tries to take it seriously even when the melodrama moves way past the point of just being ridiculous." Nevertheless, the movie marked Day's first real failure in Hollywood, and perhaps not surprisingly, she returned to her specialty, the musical comedy.

Chapter 7: Day at the Top

"I'm tired of being thought of as Miss Goody Two-Shoes... the girl next door, Miss Happy-Go-Lucky." – Doris Day

By the mid-1950s, Day was so well-known that she had her pick of leading men. Thus, after making *Pajama Game* with John Raitt in 1957, she went on to star with Clark Gable in Paramount Studio's *Teacher's Pet* in 1958. That same year she played opposite Richard Widmark in *The Tunnel of Love*. In spite of the success of these films, her next movie, *It Happened to Jane*, was not so popular, and 1958 also marked the end of the first full decade of Day being the most popular female singer in America.

However, the best was actually yet to come. In 1959, she made her first romantic comedy with Rock Hudson and Tony Randall. When Hudson was first approached about starring in the comedy *Pillow Talk*, he refused the part; in addition to not liking the script, he had never done comedy before, and he was understandably afraid that he would not be good at it. Day understood his trepidation, later explaining, "I felt he was shy and very sweet [but] I was aware of the chemistry between us…I think it was fear of the unknown, but we thought he'd be perfect and tried to reassure him."

Rock Hudson

After Hudson met Day, whose voice had enchanted him during World War II, he agreed to do the movie, and Hudson would later praise her comedic skill and timing: "Doris and I became terrific friends. She's a dynamo – a strong lady. And, boy, what a comedienne she is! The trouble was trying not to laugh. What shows on the screen, I think, is what helped make those films successful. The twinkle shows in the eyes. And we had it." Hudson later added, "Her sense of timing, her instincts. I just kept my eyes open and copied her. Doris was an actor's studio all by herself. When she cried, she cried funny, which is something I couldn't even try to explain; and when she laughed, her laughter came boiling up from her kneecaps."

The parts that the two stars played in *Pillow Talk* seemed to be written for them. Day played Janet Morrow, an interior decorator living in an elegant Manhattan apartment, while Hudson is her neighbor, Brad Allen, a songwriter with whom she shares a party line. The two are constantly locking horns over the use of the line, with Morrow unable to make business calls because Allen is always on the phone singing his latest creation to a new girl. They are often seen on-screen together, in split screen fashion, talking on the phone to each other. Of course, in the end, the two end up falling in love.

Much to everyone's surprise, the film became not only a box office hit but a gentle way to look at the sexual revolution just beginning in America at that time. Doris Day was seen as the perfectly mannered girl who, though she agreed to go on a trip with Allen, would never have considered sleeping with him. Allen, on the other hand, was seen as the randy playboy with only one thing on his mind. The fact that he ended up as a husband and future father sent a happy, comfortable message to the American public: people who stick to their morals will be all right.

While things would not necessarily turn out "all right" for every moral American in the 1950s, Hudson and Day were certainly going to do well for a while. They had a rare on-screen chemistry that audiences found irresistible, as Hudson described: "I don't really know what makes a movie team. First of all, the two people have to truly like each other, as Doris and I did, or that shines through. Then, too, both parties have to be strong personalities – very important to comedy – so that there's a tug-of-war over who's going to put it over on the other, who's going to get the last word, a fencing match between two adroit opponents of the opposite sex who in the end are going to fall into bed together."

As soon as *Pillow Talk* came out, both critics and audiences loved it, and they also loved Hudson and Day together. After she was nominated for an Academy Award for Best Actress in that film, Day quickly insisted that they do another film together, and this film, *Lover Come Back*, pushed the innuendo envelope even more. *Lover Come Back* tells the story of Carol Templeton, an unwed mother on her way to the delivery room to have her baby. The audience later learns, through flashbacks, that she had been briefly married to Jerry Webster earlier but then had the marriage annulled. Of course, viewers' sensibilities are satisfied when Webster shows up at the last minute and marries her again just before the baby is born. Like *Pillow Talk*, *Lover Come Back* was a big hit, grossing over $8 million in the United States alone. Critics loved it too, with the New York Times cooing, "Mr. Hudson and Miss Day are delicious, he in his big sprawling way and she in her wide-eyed, pert, pugnacious and eventually melting vein."

The two immediately began to look for yet another project to do together, and they found it in 1963's *Send Me No Flowers*. In this comedy of errors, they played a confused married couple struggling with a huge misunderstanding; he thinks he is dying, while she thinks he's having an affair. Unfortunately, the movie lacked the kick of their early works, and the two would not work together again for two decades, even though they remained close friends. In reference to their long association with each other, Hudson would later note in jest, "Why don't you put that in the headline: 'He Only Did Three With Doris!' Set a lot of people straight."

In addition to her string of hits with Hudson, Day appeared with Cary Grant in *That Touch of Mink* (1962), a wildly successful movie that became the first film in history to make more than $1 million in a single theatre. As a once aspiring dancer, Day must have been gratified that the theatre in question was Radio City Music Hall, home of the famous Rockettes. *That Touch of Mink* helped send Day to the top of the box office movie charts, and she later became the only woman to reach that status four times in her career. She would go on to receive 7 Laurel Awards in a row for being the most financially valuable female star in Hollywood.

Doris Day and Cary Grant in *That Touch of Mink*

In 1963, Day and James Garner starred together in *The Thrill of It All*, which had Day performing at her comedic best as a housewife who yearns to become an actress. Likewise, Garner proved to be her perfect foil as her confused and long-suffering husband, and the climactic scene of Garner driving his car into the family's new swimming pool is the stuff of Hollywood legend. Another one of the things that made *The Thrill of It All* so popular with audiences was that it brought a comedic touch to what was becoming an increasingly sensitive topic in American society. The tension in the movie surrounded Day's character wanting to do more than just be a wife and mother. Likewise, Garner did an excellent job at capturing the confused feeling that many husbands in America were having as they learned that their wives might want a career outside the home. Day knew that ultimately it was the thing people fear most that they often find funny, and the movie was full of jokes about sex and death. Audiences appreciated their work and flocked to the theaters to see *The Thrill Of It All*.

Later that year, Day and Garner teamed up again in *Move Over, Darling*, a gentle comedy about a woman who returns to her family after being declared dead. Her husband is about to remarry, but she of course wants him back, and Day gets her man in another storybook ending. The movie was all the more special to her because the theme song, "Move Over, Darling", was written by her own son. However, *Move Over, Darling* proved to be Day's last top 10 film, and today it is best remembered as being the end result of the legendary (and star-crossed) project *Something's Got to Give*, which was supposed to star Dean Martin and Marilyn Monroe but ended up being scrapped due to Monroe's erratic behavior and subsequent death.

Chapter 8: Daytime

"Nothing seems to daunt the persistent image of me as the unsullied sunshine girl.... So there must be something about me, about whatever it is that I give off, that accounts for this disparity between who I am and who I appear to be." – Doris Day

By the mid-1960s, America was in the throes of the sexual revolution, and audiences were starting to sour on pictures about "good girls" and suburban housewives. While Day briefly tried her hand once more in a drama, starring opposite Rex Harrison in a remake of *Gaslight*, she did not find non-comedic roles to her liking. At the same time, she didn't much care for parts that she considered smutty either; when she was offered the part of Mrs. Robinson in *The Graduate*, she turned it down, saying that she found the movie "vulgar and offensive."

While it's easy to admire Day for standing her moral ground, her audiences were not so appreciative. Her 1965 movie, *Do Not Disturb*, was panned by critics and avoided by her fans. Likewise, *The Glass Bottom Boat* (1966), was not the type of hit she was accustomed to. Following two more box office failures, Day made her final film, *With Six You Get Egg Roll*, in 1968.

All things considered, Day had enjoyed an incredibly successful career in the two decades she spent making movies. She received a total of nine Laurel award nominations, with four wins and four Golden Globe nominations. While she never received an Academy Award, several critics continue to lobby for an honorary Oscar for her to this day.

Unfortunately, 1968 proved to be one of the worst years in Day's life. In addition to marking the end of her film career, her husband of 17 years also died that year. Melcher had been a devout Christian Scientist who successfully brought Day into that faith, and as part of that belief system, the two eschewed medical treatment and instead relied on natural healing products and faith. In the end, Melcher may have died for his faith, possibly from a ruptured appendix.

To make bad matters worse, no sooner did Day learn that she was a widow then she learned that she was also broke. Melcher and her attorney, Jerome Rosenthal, had mismanaged her earnings so badly that her son Terry would later note that his mother would have been bankrupt had Melcher not died. To this day, it remains unclear whether Melcher was actually trying to cheat Day or if he had been duped by Rosenthal, but Day always maintained that she believed her husband had been innocent of any wrongdoing and had instead just "trusted the wrong person."

Day was heartbroken, which is understandable because she had been married to Melcher and had known Rosenthal since he represented her in her divorce from George Weilder. In spite of their past relationship, Day sued Rosenthal for what she considered his negligence and eventually won $6 million in the suit. The judge in charge of the case chastised Rosenthal for his poor management, but Rosenthal continued to file one lawsuit after another to try to get his money and reputation back. Instead, he was ultimately disbarred.

Day was even more upset when she learned that, without her permission or knowledge, Melcher had contracted her to do a television series called *The Doris Day Show*. Day would later say, "It was awful. I was really, really not very well when Marty passed away, and the thought of going into TV was overpowering. But he'd signed me up for a series. And then my son Terry took me walking in Beverly Hills and explained that it wasn't nearly the end of it. I had also been signed up for a bunch of TV specials, all without anyone ever asking me. There was a contract. I didn't know about it. I never wanted to do TV, but I gave it 100 percent anyway. That's the only way I know how to do it."

Thus, *The Doris Day Show* opened in September 1968 to the sound of Doris singing her famous "Que Sera, Sera." While Day did not like doing the series and later complained that she was "delivered to CBS", the public would never have known because she was all smiles on air. At the same time, she insisted that CBS allow her and Terry creative control of the show, which posed a problem because neither of them had any television experience. Rather than take a concept and work to improve it, they were constantly changing both the premise and the cast of the show. While the show was not overwhelmingly popular, it did help pay off the debts her husband had accrued, and it also provided the inspiration for *The Carol Burnett Show*. After *The Doris Day Show* went off the air, aside from appearing in two TV specials, Day would not return to either the big screen or the small screen for another decade.

Chapter 9: Later Years

"I never retired." – Doris Day

After the death of her husband, Day became even more attached to her pets. She had always enjoyed the company of dogs since Tiny's faithful company during her recovery from her accident, and as she became more aware of how animals around the world were being treated, Day decided to do something to raise funds and awareness of their plight, vowing, "I'm going to do as much as I can for the animal world, and I'll never stop." To that end, she co-founded Actors and Others for Animals in 1971, and she also appeared with Mary Tyler Moore, Angie Dickinson and others in newspaper ads criticizing people for wearing furs. Her activism was detailed by Cleveland Amory in 1974 in *Man Kind? Our Incredible War on Wildlife* (1974), and as she explained, "I've never met an animal I didn't like, and I can't say the same thing about people."

Four years later, Day created her own organization, the Doris Day Pet Foundation (now the Doris Day Animal Foundation). The DDAF awards grants and monetary assistance to organizations in the United States that seek to help animals and those who care for them, and despite her advanced age, Day continues to supervise the day-to-day operation of the foundation, explaining, "I just love that I can make it better for the animals. I know I have – for far – with my pet foundation. That is thrilling for me."

As an animal activist in the early 1980s, Day had one advantage that most other lobbyists could only dream of. When she was concerned about pending legislation, she just picked up the phone and called the White House. Upon identifying herself, she was always put straight through to the President of the United States, her old co-star in *The Winning Team*, Ronald Reagan. Rumor has long had it that the two of them had an affair several decades earlier, but regardless of the veracity of it, they were clearly on good terms. Toward the end of Reagan's second term in office, Day decided to formalize her lobbying by forming the Doris Day Animal League in 1987. As the legislative arm of her Animal Foundation, its purpose is to work to pass laws to protect animals in the United States and around the world.

In 1976, Day married for the fourth and final time. This time the groom was Barry Comden, a man 10 years her junior who met Day while he was working as the maître d' at a restaurant she frequented. When he heard how much Day doted on her dogs, he began to send her home from her dinners there with bones and meat scraps for her canine friends. That said, Comden's behavior seems in keeping with the classic "gold digger" model, and he and Day were only married for a few years before divorcing in 1981, the same year that Day was inducted in the Women's Hall of Fame in her home state of Ohio.

After she divorced Comden, Day moved to Carmel-by-the-Sea, California, where she bought a hotel called The Cypress Inn. From the beginning, Day wanted her hotel to be unique and to cater to her fellow animal lovers who wanted to travel with their pets. The Cypress Inn not only allowed pets, it also catered to them by offering on-site pet sitting services.

In 1985, Day returned once more to television with the short lived *Doris Day's Best Friends Show*. Airing on Pat Robertson's Christian Broadcasting Network, Day's success may have been hampered by her choice in "Best Friends." Her first guest was long time pal Rock Hudson, who was clearly very ill during the filming of the episode but insisted on making what would be his last television appearance. Within months, the world learned that he was dying of AIDS, and that he had been an active member of California's gay community for most of his life. Due to a lack of understanding and fear over the AIDS epidemic in the '80s, Hudson soon became the poster child for the disease, and the network cancelled Day's show at the end of its first season.

The older Day became, the less she liked to travel, and this was most notable in 1989, when she agreed to join Patrick Swayze and Marvin Hamlish in presenting the Oscar for Best Original Score at the 61st Annual Academy Awards. However, she backed out at the last moment, citing a leg injury; she was apparently out walking on the grounds of The Cypress Inn when she bumped into a sprinkler and badly cut her leg. While this story was likely true, it seems that she still could have made the awards dinner had she wanted to.

As the nostalgic era of the 1980s wore on, people began to once more take notice of Day's work. She received the Cecil B. DeMille Award for career achievement in 1989, and after being encouraged by friends, Day released a Greatest Hits album in 1994. While it was only moderately well-received in the United States, it became a big hit in Great Britain. In fact, a song from the album, "Perhaps, Perhaps, Perhaps" became part of the soundtrack for an Australian film titled *Strictly Ballroom*. The same song was also the theme song for the critically acclaimed British comedy *Coupling*.

While such recognition is always welcome, Doris Day had already received plenty of accolades, and it seems that Day appreciates the recognition mostly to the extent that it allows her to keep helping her furry friends. In 1995, Day used her clout to encourage Congress to pass laws to protect the safety and welfare of animals, which led to Congress designating an annual "Spay Day USA."

Awards continued to pour in for Day throughout the first decade of the 21st century. In 2000, the State of Ohio awarded her its highest civilian award, the Ohio Medal of Honor, and a few years later, in 2004, Day received the Presidential Medal of Freedom by President George W. Bush. The medal not only recognized Day's work as an entertainer but also acknowledged her efforts on behalf of animals. In his speech at the award ceremony, President Bush noted, "It was a good day for our fellow creatures when she gave her good heart to the cause of animal welfare." For her part, Day expressed amazement that she was being honored, saying, "My first reaction was, `For what?' I'm not being coy, or looking for a laugh. I have never thought about awards, whatever I do." She went on to express another reaction: fear of flying that she picked up while touring with Bob Hope. "I am deeply grateful to the president and to my country. But I won't fly. Bob would fly even if a cyclone was coming. I saw him on his knees many a time. In fact, we were all on our knees. We flew in snowstorms, whatever, to get to the next show. When I hit the ground, I said, 'Never again.'"

Sadly, Day had other, more private reasons for not wanting to leave California at this time: her only son was dying of cancer. Terry passed away in November 2004, leaving behind his wife and Day's only grandchild, his son Ryan.

Though now in her 80s, Day continued to work well into the new century. In 2006, she provided taped commentary for the DVDs of the final season of her television show, and that same year, she merged her Animal League with The Humane Society in the United States. She coordinated the merger herself, with members of her organization joining the Humane Society, and she personally recorded public service announcements supporting the organization, especially World Spay Day. She was inducted into the Hit Parade Hall of Fame in 2007.

Day continues to give telephone interviews to radio stations on her birthday, and in 2008 she made a rare on-air appearance with her friend George Putnam. However, Day still turned down honors from both the American Film Institute and the Kennedy Center because she did not want to travel across country to receive them. The same was true when she won a Grammy for Lifetime Achievement in Music in 2008. Fortunately, the Grammy committee was more flexible and gave her the award anyway, to go along with the other three Grammys she won during her lifetime for "Sentimental Journey" (1998), "Secret Love" (1999) and "Que Sera, Sera" (2012).

In 2010, Day became the first person to receive the Legend Award from the Society of Singers, but the legend wasn't done working. The following year, she released another album of brand new material, *My Heart*, the first new album she had come out with in almost 20 years. *My Heart* contained songs that Terry Melcher had produced during the 1970s, and there were also several of Day's old jazz pieces, including "My Buddy," which she dedicated to her son's memory:

"Life is a book that we study

Some of its leaves bring a sigh

There it was written by a buddy

That we must part, you and I

Nights are long since you went away

I think about you all through the day

My buddy, my buddy

Nobody quite so true

Miss your voice, the touch of your hand

Just long to know that you understand

My buddy, my buddy

Your buddy misses you

Your buddy misses you, yes I do"

The CD was released on December 6, and its haunting melodies resonated with Americans missing people and better times during Christmas. Within two weeks, it was #12 on Amazon's Best Seller list, and it also reached the 135th slot on the Billboard, the first of Day's recordings to make the chart since 1963. The album also made Day the oldest artist to make it to a Top 10 slot in the United Kingdom with an album of new material. Of course, most of the money the album made went to fund Day's work on behalf of animals, including the Doris Day Horse Rescue and Adoption Center in Murchison, Texas. That facility was opened by Day in 2011 on land once owned by fellow animal lover Cleveland Amory.

In 2012, Day earned her latest honor, a Lifetime Achievement Award from the Los Angeles Film Critics Association. There's no telling what the future would bring, but as Doris Day's life and career suggest, anything is possible.

Bibliography

Barothy, Mary Anne. Day at a Time: An Indiana Girl's Sentimental Journey to Doris Day's Hollywood and Beyond (2013)

Braun, Eric. Doris Day (2004)

Bret, David. Doris Day: A Reluctant Star (2009)

DeVita, Michael. My "Secret Love" Affair with Doris Day (2012)

Freeland, Michael. Doris Day: The Illustrated Biography (2000)

Hotchner, A.E. Doris Day: Her Own Story (1976)

Kaufman, David. Doris Day: The Untold Story of the Girl Next Door (2010)

McDonald, Tamar Jeffers. Doris Day Confidential: Hollywood, Sex and Stardom (2013)

McGee, Garry. Doris Day: Sentimental Journey (2010)

Patrick, Pierre, Garry McGee and Jackie Joseph. The Doris Day Companion: A Beautiful Day (2009)

Santopietro, Tom. Considering Doris Day (2008)

Young, Christopher. The Films of Doris Day (1977)

Printed in Great Britain
by Amazon